# The Moment I FELL!

Carmen Gonzalez

Copyright © (2026) Carmen Gonzalez

All rights reserved. No portion of this book may be reproduced or transmitted by any means-electronic, mechanical, photocopy, recording, or otherwise without the prior written permission of the copyright owner.

Carmen Gonzalez

Email: Writingmovesme@gmail.com

ISBN: 979-8-9988627-0-0

Editor: Abigail L. Gonzalez

# Table of Contents

Dedication ................................................................. 1

Introduction .............................................................. 4

Chapter One: Routinely Awakened ................................. 8

Chapter Two: The Kiss of Death ..................................... 12

Chapter Three: Stepping Away ........................................ 18

Chapter Four: Finding Me ............................................... 21

Chapter Five: The Truth in Manifestation ....................... 24

Chapter Six: Life Beyond the Usual ................................ 29

Chapter Seven: God's Direction in Guiding Who You Are ................................................................................ 34

   PRAYER BREAK ...................................................... 38

Chapter Eight: Whose Breath You Bear .......................... 42

Chapter Nine: When the Spirit Hungers .......................... 49

Chapter Ten: When Destiny Calls Your Name ................ 53

Chapter Eleven: Walking in Your New Identity .............. 56

Chapter Twelve: The Whisper That Leads the Way ......... 59

Chapter Thirteen: Becoming Who God Saw All Along ... 65

Chapter Fourteen: When Faith Stands in the Fire ............ 69

Chapter Fifteen: A Life that Shines ................................. 74

Chapter Sixteen: The Power of Persistent Prayer ............ 78

Chapter Seventeen: When God Turns Waiting into Becoming ...................................................................... 84

Chapter Eighteen: Walking in God's Peace ..................... 88

Closing .......................................................................... 94

The AMEN to Your Becoming

## **Dedication**

This journey is about growth, renewal, and the courage to rise. I hope that you will embrace your unique story, find strength in your voice, and take bold steps toward the dreams that have long lived within you. May this be a space where we uplift one another, share wisdom, and celebrate progress in all its forms, whether monumental or small.

You deserve joy, purpose, and fulfillment. As I share the path that led me toward healing and clarity, I invite you to allow your own story to unfold. I would be honored to hear how you have overcome challenges, broken cycles, and step confidently into who you are becoming. I want these words to reach every heart in need of encouragement, because no one should sacrifice their well-being for the sake of others' comfort. I learned that lesson painfully, that you cannot pour from an empty cup, nor can you live fully while neglecting your own soul.

Together, we can explore the transformative power of self-love, acceptance, and emotional honesty. It is okay, truly okay, to put yourself first, to recognize your needs, and to feel what you feel without apology. We are often pressured to wear a mask, but real joy grows from authenticity and self-compassion. As I share the tools that helped me heal, like journaling, meditation, intention setting, and professional support, I hope they provide you with guidance and peace. Each practice played a role in helping me reclaim my life, and they can help you reclaim yours.

I have come to understand that every setback carries the seed of a comeback, and that the darkest moments often reveal our deepest resilience. It wasn't until I reached the bottom that I finally saw the value of my journey and the strength that hardship had been shaping within me.

In these pages, I share my story of perseverance, its highs, lows, and the quiet victories that built the foundation of the person I am today.

# **Introduction**

This book was born from my life—my falls, my failures, and the quiet victories that rose from the ashes. It took hitting the ground to understand my place, and it took breaking to discover what could be rebuilt. In the moments when I dropped to my knees in prayer, trembling with questions I was afraid to voice, I found answers. In that sacred solitude, I uncovered the fragments of myself buried beneath years of doubt, fear, and pretending to be strong. Even my breath became proof of my resilience. In the shadows, I confronted my vulnerabilities, and in that discomfort, clarity slowly emerged.

*I learned that strength doesn't always roar; sometimes it whispers in the stillness.*

But when I stood up without prayer, when I tried living on my own terms, disconnected from God, I fell apart. I had to die within to discover my worth. Alone and confused, I sank deeper into darkness, and everything collapsed. Only then did I realize that every experience, even the painful ones, had come to shape me, to teach me, to prepare me. My path had purpose, even when it felt like punishment.

Through the darkness, a light finally broke through, a flicker of hope that sparked a fire inside me. I stopped begging for approval and began learning to approve of myself. With each challenge, I gathered the shattered pieces of my identity and stitched them back together with intention. I saw that the opinions of others did not shape my value; my worth was woven into how I loved, fought, and rose again. I dared to embrace my imperfections, to celebrate my uniqueness, and to step into the world whole and unapologetic.

Today, as I stand taller than I ever have, I understand that self-discovery is not a destination but a lifelong journey. The lessons learned guided me through every uncertainty ahead.

No longer hiding in the shadows of doubt, I walk boldly in the light of my truth.

Looking back, I realize God was calling me long before I was ready to answer. He tried to pull me from situations that were slowly destroying me, but I clung tightly to what I believed was my "good thing." I ignored the warnings. I convinced myself I was fine, that I had control. But inside, I was disappearing, losing self-esteem, losing direction, losing God.

It wasn't until the day I fell completely, emotionally, that I saw the truth. I was drowning in depression, trapped in a life that offered me nothing but emptiness. I couldn't move. I couldn't breathe.

And yet, that breaking point became my turning point. I finally understood that something can look good and still not be right. When I acknowledged that truth, I found freedom. And this book is the story of how I rose, not perfectly, not instantly, but faithfully, into the woman I was always meant to become.

# **Chapter One**

## **Routinely Awakened**

I didn't realize I was asleep until God started shaking the pieces of my life that no longer fit His plan. My days were stitched together with distractions, small, constant, numbing. I woke up with them. Ate breakfast beside them. Carried them through the week as though they were necessary to my survival. My calendar stayed full, but my life stayed empty. I called it productivity, but it was only noise, noise that kept me from hearing God. Weekends blend into chores, errands, and excuses. Busyness became my badge of honor.

I chased relevance, chased affirmation, chased anything that made me feel like I mattered. Yet the more I chased, the more anxious I became. My relationships cracked under the weight of my *distraction*. My mind wandered even while my body stayed present. And one night, as I stared at a reflection

I didn't recognize, the truth finally struck me: I was living on autopilot, drifting toward a life I didn't want.

The routine had swallowed me whole. And then came *he*. My *distraction* disguised as a significant other. I accepted crumbs and called it commitment. I normalized emotional starvation and called it love. I ignored wise counsel because I feared letting go more than I feared losing myself.

Unequally yoked, I tied my spirit to someone who dimmed it daily. "It doesn't take all that to go to heaven," he'd say, and I believed him because it was easier than confronting the truth. I lost myself in sweet lies and practiced denial like a ritual. Everyone saw the danger but me.

Still, I stayed. Stayed because attention felt like affection, and loneliness felt worse than his half-love. Stayed until I no longer recognized the woman staring back at me, until my sons became my only reason to breathe.

I watched as even they were slowly deceived by his mask, and still I covered *him*. Still, I excused *him*.

The emotional, mental, and spiritual abuse wore me down until my truth broke into pieces. I silenced my instincts, defended his behavior, and betrayed myself in the name of love. My heart wanted him, but my soul was suffocating. I sought escape in alcohol, isolation, and silence. Depression settled in like a fog. The mirror became a stranger. My smile faded, and survival became my only mission.

I prayed without sound, "Help me," a cry I didn't dare say aloud. Life became a cycle of pretending: working, cooking, cleaning, mothering. Physically, I felt unworthy. Mentally, I was unraveling. Spiritually, I was starving.

Hospital visits became routine, my body keeping record of what my heart refused to acknowledge. Pills became the bandages for wounds I wouldn't name. Each symptom was a sermon my body preached: *Leave before it destroys you.*

But fear gripped me. The unknown felt larger than the pain I already knew. I hid from friends, family, and my own truth. Anything was easier than admitting the love I fought for was slowly killing me.

I thought I had built a life, but all I had built was a prison. I gave it decor and returned willingly. What I thought was a relationship turned out to be **the kiss of death**.

And that is the moment God began preparing to resurrect me.

## Chapter Two

## The Kiss of Death

Every woman longs to be loved rightly, yet sometimes the hunger for love becomes the very doorway through which pain walks in. Women desire safety, tenderness, and a place to rest their hearts. To be understood, valued, prioritized, and cherished like the jewels God designed us to be. I wanted the kind of love people testified about, the kind you feel deep in your soul, the kind that brings peace instead of confusion.

But instead of love, I settled for the shadow of it. I didn't fall for a man, I fell for potential. For what *could be*. For a future he never intended to build. The bare minimum became my daily bread. What he desired ruled my world, and my needs became an inconvenience. Anytime I desired moments with my family, his response was always the same: *"What about me? Who's going to spend time with me?"*

Slowly, his selfishness carved pieces out of me. I wasn't his partner. I had become his possession. A silent ornament in a life where my happiness didn't matter. What I thought was love weakened me at the root. His gaslighting turned his betrayals into my so-called failures. He stood tall as the victim while I became guilty for things I didn't do. And still he kept me close with gifts.

There were fancy dinner reservations, clothes, and shoes. Affection wrapped in material things, hoping I'd forget the fractures in my heart. And the worst part? I accepted it. I covered and carried him while I silenced myself so he could shine. Looking back, I can honestly say I had lowered my standards so he could stay. I gave everything while receiving nothing that fed my spirit. I believed I couldn't live without him.

My plans, events, and dreams all fell aside if he decided we had something "better" to do. Even my birthday became a battlefield. I told my sons I wanted to see the wax museum in New York City, but he insisted on his own plans. When I reminded him that my sons would be joining us, his anger rose like a storm. He wanted my birthday to belong to *him*— even if it meant excluding the children who had given my life purpose.

And when he couldn't control the plan, he made it the wound he would reopen for a year. The ruined birthday. The missed proposal. The "special plans" I supposedly ruined.

Empty apologies followed, but deep down, I knew it wasn't the end of his manipulation; it was just the intermission. I wanted to escape, but the chains of guilt held me. I convinced myself that if I tried harder, loved deeper, gave more, he would finally treat me right. That one day, he'd wake up and see my worth. Instead, I started blaming myself. I regretted not giving more of my time, my energy, my soul.

I became responsible for his happiness, while mine withered in silence. Then someone looked at me and said, "You seem like a trophy girlfriend." Confused, I asked, Why? "Because you're beautiful, stable, and put together. It makes you the kind of woman a man wants on his arm to look good."

And suddenly, the puzzle pieces shifted. He didn't love me. He loved the image of me. He loved how I made him appear. I recalled one conversation where he joked with a friend that I'd take care of him when he was old, that I'd still be full of life when he was seventy. He laughed, brushed it off, kissed my forehead, kissed my lips, and that kiss, soft and familiar, **was the kiss of death.**

It wasn't affection. It was control disguised as tenderness. A trap wrapped in sweetness. He used that kiss to pull me back. To confuse my heart. To make me forget the pain. And for a moment, I did. My lips touched his, and the lies tasted like comfort.

But this time, something felt different. As he leaned back and asked, "Are you okay?" I touched my lips and felt the weight of a decision forming in my spirit. Would I keep allowing myself to be deceived? Or would I choose to walk away from the very thing that was slowly destroying me?

My heart was torn between the desire to stay and the calling to run. Between the trap and the truth. Between his voice and the whisper of God saying, *"You deserve more than this."*

I reminded myself of the reality 99.9% of the time, I felt unheard, dismissed, and invisible. I was sinking in a ship that had been sinking long before I climbed aboard. I kept telling myself I was meant to fix him, to build him, to carry his brokenness as if it were my assignment.

But why?

What about my heart, my peace, and the woman God called me to be? Leaving wasn't selfish. Staying was the betrayal, a betrayal of my own worth. So how does someone leave a man who is killing them softly?

*You stop kissing death and start choosing life.*

## Chapter Three

## Stepping Away

Sleepless nights became a rhythm I never asked for. A quiet war waged in the dark as I wrestled with the decision that would redirect the very course of my life. The pain tightened its grip. Confusion clouded my mind. From the bottom, I longed to sink, to disappear beneath the weight of what my heart could no longer carry. I was trapped between what hurt me and what I still loved. And there, in the tension, God whispered what I did not want to admit: *"If you stay, you will wither."*

I would become a memory instead of a miracle in motion. I tried to imagine the pain away, but fantasy could no longer mask the truth. What I needed was healing from rejection, from the ache that clung like a shadow, from the emptiness that begged for attention to soothe it. Still, I stood, trembling, waiting for deliverance to find me.

I reminded myself: *I am better than this.* Remaining in this wreck was a choice only I could undo. Would I run toward restoration, or cling to the illusion I had crafted so carefully? My body felt drained, slumped in surrender. So there, with a weary heart, I whispered, "Lord, I need to rest. I need clarity. I need peace."

As sleep overtook me, something shifted. I drifted upward above the clouds, above the ache, above the shame. In that dream, I stood as a witness to my own freedom. Rejection loosened its grip, and hope rose like the sun.

A smile, unexpected and pure, warmed my face. It was the confirmation I had begged heaven for. The next morning, it was different. Affection misplaced for too long was finally returned home. My desire to heal became my anchor. My "why" was born in the night. Ready to rebuild, to restore the parts of my soul I had abandoned. Never would I submit to the familiar pain that tried to claim me. I faced the mirror, inhaled deeply, and spoke life into my reflection: "I got this. I made it. I am amazing."

In that moment, I felt proud—proud of who I was becoming, proud of the smile that met me each morning, proud of the peace I had cultivated with my own two hands and God's grace.

One day at a time, I stepped into a journey of rediscovery. I welcomed the quiet victories. I learned from the missteps. I celebrated my strength. My decisions mattered, my needs mattered, and I explored passions I had silenced in the past. I allowed myself to create, to dream, and to breathe without judgment.

Mistakes became teachers. Every moment became a lesson. And slowly, steadily, joy returned, one gentle sunrise at a time. And there it was, the truth I thought I had lost:

***I was learning to love myself again.***

## Chapter Four

## Finding Me

I trembled at the start of my new journey, but every morning I dropped to my knees, letting my prayers rise before I did. I asked God for direction—for strength to stand, strength to breathe, strength to begin again. And each time I whispered my petitions, a quiet comfort wrapped around me, reminding me I was not walking alone. "Woman, look at you," I told myself. "Look at your glow." That radiance wasn't man-made; it was heaven-sent. It was Jesus restoring what life tried to strip from me.

Day by day, God steadied my steps. My whispered prayer became Psalm 25:4-5, my compass in the wilderness. I felt His nearness again, fear dissolved, courage awakened, and my hunger for Him returned.

Church became my refuge, prayer my oxygen, Scripture my anchor. The closer I drew to Him, the more I recognized the woman He always intended me to be. Romans 8 reminded me that destiny had never lost my name. So, I began dating myself. Learning my likes, honoring my needs, tending to my body like a sacred garden. Spa days, fresh hair, quiet dinners, long walks, and moments of softness healed parts of me I didn't know were bruised. I discovered that loving myself was not selfish; it was stewardship. It was obedience. It was worship. Self-care became my sanctuary.

I poured into myself because an empty cup cannot overflow. Jesus became my first love, and from that love, I became whole. I worked out, I breathed deeper, I lived lighter. My mind cleared. My heart steadied. The weight of old wounds fell off me like chains breaking at His command.

I shifted my lifestyle with new habits, clean eating, more water, and more discipline. My skin brightened, my energy bloomed, and my soul exhaled.

I committed to strengthening every part of me: physically, mentally, spiritually, and emotionally. Excellence became my language. Purpose became my pace. People noticed—"You look happy." "You look free." And I was. Free in God. Free in truth. Free in identity. Free in grace.

When I finally let go, God opened the floodgates. Blessings overtook me, favor found me, and peace embraced me. Isaiah 54:17 proved itself true. I was unbroken, unshaken, unstoppable. What tried to destroy me only shaped me. What tried to silence me only sharpened me.

I surrounded myself with visionaries, dreamers, builders, and people who stretched me, inspired me, and elevated me. My goals grew. My standards rose. My excuses died. Each day became an invitation to greatness.

And in the quiet strength of my becoming, I finally saw it. I was not just finding myself; I was finding the woman God had always designed me to be.

# Chapter Five

## The Truth in Manifestation

There is a sacred power in speaking what your eyes cannot yet see. Manifestation became the language of my faith. I walked through the doors of my condo one afternoon and declared aloud, "This is the year I will move into my house." I didn't whisper it. I didn't hope it. I **announced** it.

Intentionally, boldly, with Heaven as my witness. I prayed specifically for a four-bedroom, two-bathroom home. Every day, I thanked God as though the keys were already in my hands. My faith became so alive that I began to pack without a forwarding address, without an approval letter, without any physical evidence. I knew—*it was time, and my house was already waiting for me.*

Scripture reminded me of what my spirit felt. *"Now faith is the substance of things hoped for, the evidence of things not seen."* (Heb. 11:1). I could not see the house, but my faith saw it clearly. I prayed and prepared. I saved intentionally. I packed lunches instead of buying them. I refused to spend money on anything that didn't align with the vision God had for me.

I began the process. House after house, prayer after prayer, rejection letters after another. The first offer—denied. The second—outbid. A younger version of me would have cried. But the healed version whispered, "If God shut the door, it wasn't mine." I didn't mourn opportunities that weren't aligned with Heaven's blueprint.

Three months later, I stepped into *my* home—before I even knew it was mine. My son and I walked through the rooms, already planning where joy would live, where peace would sit, where dreams would grow. My heart settled. My spirit stood still. And I said, **"This is it. I'll take it."**

When I asked my realtor to submit the offer with the seller's assist, believing the seller would agree to pay a portion of my closing costs, she hesitated. "It's almost impossible," she warned. But I smiled gently and said, "Submit it anyway. God is in this."

Three days later, I was approved. But the conditions felt impossible. The seller was asking for more money down, with more proof of income. I looked at my bank account, then lifted my eyes and said, "God, You did not bring me this far to leave me. I thank You for provision from the north, south, east, and west."

And just as I prayed, the money began to flow in. It was **unexpected**, **unexplainable**, and **all God**.

At closing, the unexpected continued. The down payment costs dropped, and refunds appeared. Favor overflowed. I walked out of that office with keys in my hand and tears in my eyes. God had proven Himself faithful again. *"Ask, and it shall be given"* (Matt. 7:7-8). I asked. I sought. I knocked. And God opened.

But God wasn't done yet.

Months before, while walking the streets of Miami with my sister Abigail, I saw a blue Mustang convertible glide past us. "One day," I said, "I'm going to have one just like that."

She looked back at me and asked, "Why not now?"

I laughed it off. "My SUV is fine. I don't need another car."

She stopped walking, looked me straight in the eyes, and said, "You will never step into something new while clinging to what feels comfortable. Sometimes God has to push you into your new."

I didn't know how prophetic her words were.

When I returned home from my trip in Miami, my SUV was involved in an accident—no injuries, but the vehicle was no longer drivable. Suddenly, comfort was gone. Choice was gone. And the Holy Spirit whispered, *"You wouldn't have moved unless you had no choice."*

I searched online. Three days later, there it was. The exact blue Mustang convertible I had spoken into the atmosphere. When I walked into the dealership, the salesman said, "It's been sitting here for weeks."

I replied with confidence, "That's because it's my car."

And that same day, I drove off the lot in my dream car—top down, wind blowing, heart full. God did it again.

My faith grew roots, and my relationship with God became personal. I vowed never to shrink under someone else's fear or doubt. I had witnessed impossible things bend under the weight of God's favor. You cannot tell me God is not real—I have lived the proof.

My life belongs to Him. My trust belongs to Him. And now, my future walks in the light of a God who never fails.

# Chapter Six

## Life Beyond the Usual

Surrounded by melodies that lifted my spirit, I began to fill my heart with music that breathed life instead of chaos. I remembered when my thoughts were shaped by the songs I allowed into my mind, like rap music that was filled with profanity, pride, and violence. Soon, those lyrics became my language. My speech hardened. My reactions sharpened. My heart grew restless. I realized that if I continued feeding my spirit poison, I would eventually walk a poisoned path.

So, I became intentional.

With purpose, I changed the soundtrack of my life. I turned to inspirational music—songs that reminded me of who God is and who I was becoming. One of my favorites, "Mighty Name of Jesus," echoed through my home like a declaration: *He has all authority over my life.* The more I listened, the more peace took residence. The more I sought God, the more my lifestyle shifted. I became aware of the company I kept, the places I visited, and the atmosphere I entered. If I were to walk with God, every aspect of my life needed alignment.

I realized that the Holy Spirit works with each of us in different ways. For me, He started with my words. Proverbs 18:21 says, "Death and life are in the power of the tongue." I witnessed how words carried weight—shaping emotions, influencing decisions, building futures, or destroying them. If I wanted change, it had to begin within me.

Someone once asked, "Why is your face glowing? What new product are you using?" I smiled and said, "Nothing changed but the decision to follow God wholeheartedly." My walk became steady. My joy was renewed. Freedom had reached my mind, then my heart, and finally my actions.

God desires for us to be free spiritually, mentally, physically, and emotionally. John 8:36 reminds us, *"If the Son therefore shall make you free, ye shall be free indeed."*

Freedom has no monetary cost. It simply begins with a decision to trust God and surrender the outcome to Him.

So, I ask you: Are you free today? Do you live without fear? Are you being fully yourself? Freedom isn't about religion or tradition; it's a mindset shift, a willingness to embrace growth, and a decision to stop living by others' expectations. When you find your place and discover your true self, confidence naturally rises. When you walk in the freedom of Christ, the opinions of others no longer imprison you.

Living in God's embrace brings goodness into your life. When you prioritize God, freedom naturally follows. Guard your spirit. Be intentional about whose presence you enter. It took time for me to recognize how real spiritual warfare is, but once you choose Christ, the enemy will attempt to disturb your peace through any willing vessel.

Pay attention to this:

"There is a target on your life. For the enemy seeks to destroy you. Be watchful. Pray. Live in the authority God has given you. Let Him order your steps. Forsake the past so He can renew you. Trouble will come. Guard your life—God's got you. The road may seem lonely, the pace may be painful, but trust God—He knows."

Choosing God begins within, a quiet surrender, an honest acknowledgement that without Him we are nothing. It is in Him we live, move, and have our being. Life itself is held together by His breath. With Him, all things are possible. One of the greatest blessings of serving God is this: **He calls us His friend.**

We are family with Christ. And family is protected.

I am determined to let God lead the next chapter of my life. I honor my past, but I will not allow it to imprison me. Isaiah 55:8-9 reminds me why: *"For my thoughts are not your thoughts... my ways are higher than your ways."*

Being guided by the Holy Spirit keeps my soul at peace. I can honestly say, I am no longer afraid. My life is rooted in purpose, and the same is true for you. It is not by accident that you are reading this chapter at this exact moment in time. Maybe you're feeling overwhelmed. Maybe depressed. Maybe you've thought about giving up. Please hear me—God cares for you deeply. He wants you close. He wants to turn things around. Your past doesn't determine your future.

Release it.

Step into freedom.

Let God show you the life beyond the usual.

## Chapter Seven

## God's Direction in Guiding Who You Are

The battle of identity does not begin around us; it begins **within us**. Before a word is spoken or a step is taken, the heart quietly shapes the life that follows. Proverbs 4:23 says, *"Keep thy heart with all diligence; for out of it are the issues of life."* Every emotion, every fear, every moment of courage settles first in the heart.

What lives in the heart eventually lives in your hands, decisions, habits, and your destiny. Our hearts carry an entire world: joy and sorrow, peace and frustration, faith and doubt. We are not wrong for feeling; we are human. But we are **transformed** when we allow God to touch what we feel. When you know who you are in Christ, it does not remove your emotions; it **reorders them**, aligns them, and redeems them. Jesus invites us into clarity, not confusion.

In Matthew 7:7-8, Jesus says to ask, seek, and find, because understanding is never found outside of Him. It is God who uncovers what we hide, who heals what we protect, and who restores what we lost. He desires a relationship deep enough that nothing within us remains untouched.

When you stand before God, you do not stand as a mistake, a failure, or an afterthought. You stand as **His image-bearer**. Genesis 1:27 says it without hesitation: you were crafted on purpose, with purpose, for purpose. And 1 Peter 2:9 confirms it further: *You are chosen. You are royal. You are set apart. You are called to shine.*

So, hear this clearly: **you are not accidental.** Not your birth. Not your timing. Not your existence. God wanted you here. Your story is still in His hands. But while the heart carries our emotions, the **mind** carries our battles. And the enemy knows exactly where to aim. Romans 12:2 commands us to renew our minds because the mind is the battlefield where defeat or victory begins.

If the enemy can poison your thoughts, he can limit your steps. If he confuses your identity, he can distract your destiny. This is why your first thoughts matter. This is why affirmations matter. This is why starting your day with God is starting with armor.

Proverbs 23:7 reminds us, *"For as he thinketh in his heart, so is he."* What you repeat, you become. What you meditate on, you attract. What you believe, you eventually live.

I've carried a phrase with me through the years by Henry Ford that quotes, **"Whether you think you can, or you think you can't—you're right.**

It is simple, but it is spiritual. Faith begins as a thought, a whisper in the mind that grows into obedience.

Friend, you cannot run to everyone for everything. People may comfort you, but only God can **transform** you. Only God can reshape what you thought was permanent. As the Potter, He never loses patience with the clay. He molds, presses, stretches, and holds — all to reveal what He already saw in you from the beginning.

Saying **"yes"** to God is where it all begins. He is the doorway. The moment you say yes, the Father responds with love that carries no condemnation.

*John 3:16-17 is the heartbeat of this invitation, not to judge you, but to save, reclaim, and draw you close.*

God wants to show you what real love looks like, not the fragile, conditional love the world gives, but the steady, unfailing love that outlasts storms. Life may bruise you, but it cannot break what God is restoring. Psalm 30:5 whispers a promise to every weary soul: *"Weeping may endure for a* night, but joy cometh in the morning." And when God says morning is coming, nothing can stop it.

### PRAYER BREAK

*Lord, You see **US** fully — every misstep, every fear, every moment we've doubted You. Order our steps. Lead us where You desire us to go. Reveal Your plan, renew our hearts, cleanse our thoughts. Father, we surrender the confusion and the wandering. Thank You for sending Your Son so we may walk in grace, walk in purpose, and walk in freedom. Amen.*

Now breathe — you made it. You said yes. And Heaven heard you. Prepare yourself. God is not just leading you — He is **equipping** you and dressing you with new armor.

### The Armor You Must Wear

Ephesians 6:11-18 calls us to be dressed for a spiritual war we may not always see, but always fight. Your battle is not against people; it is against darkness that cannot stand the God within you.

**1. The Belt of Truth**

Truth holds everything together and steadies the wandering heart. Truth silences the lies the enemy whispers. As a belt secures the body, truth secures identity.

**2. The Breastplate of Righteousness**

Guard your heart. Guard your purity. Guard your intentions. A vulnerable heart becomes an easy target, but righteousness shields what matters most.

**3. Feet Fitted with the Gospel of Peace**

Peace is your anchor. Peace is your stability. Peace keeps you ready for whatever may come. Biblical soldiers wore sandals that gripped the ground — peace helps your spirit do the same.

## 4. The Shield of Faith

Faith deflects every dart aimed to wound you. Doubt cannot attach where faith stands firm. When life throws arrows, faith answers with assurance: **"God is with me."**

## 5. The Helmet of Salvation

Your mind must be guarded and your thoughts protected. Your identity must be secured. Salvation covers your mind the same way a helmet covers a soldier's head, with strength and intention.

## 6. The Sword of the Spirit — the Word of God

This is your weapon. Scripture is not meant for decoration; it is a powerful tool for defense. When faced with an enemy, instead of reacting emotionally, rely on the truth of Scripture to guide your actions.

## Stand Ready

Be grounded in God. Be available to His voice. Be alert to His leading. Life will bring both peace and pressure, but God will always be with you through it all. With Him, you will not break or lose, your story will unfold precisely as Heaven intended.

*__Be ready. Stay ready. Your steps are ordered, and your purpose is waiting.__*

## Chapter Eight

## Whose Breath You Bear

*Before you ever spoke a word, Heaven whispered your name — and all of creation already knew who you were.*

The body armor you wear is the beginning of your journey with Jesus Christ. 1 Corinthians 15:58 states, *"Therefore, my beloved brethren, be ye steadfast, unmovable, always abounding in the work of the Lord, forasmuch as ye know that your labour is not in vain in the Lord."* You are always moving, always experiencing attacks. Someone will always disagree with you or have a problem with you. Someone will always find something to say against you. There will always be someone who dislikes you and everything that you stand for.

Understand that attacks will come; how you handle them is the important part. Guard yourself by being fluent in His Word. It is one thing to say something, another to do or live it.

As stated in the last chapter, having the whole armor of God takes practice and discipline. If you purpose in your heart to serve God, He will be with you every step of the way. That is a promise that He Himself has given to us. Deuteronomy 31:6 says it better: "Be strong and of a good courage, fear not, nor be afraid of them: for the Lord thy God, He it is that doth go with thee; He will not fail thee, nor forsake thee." God will always protect you and lead you and guide you. Even at times when it doesn't feel like He is around, He is indeed there.

Who are you? Not what defines you, but who are you? Many find it difficult to answer the question because of their title and their responsibilities. Many have lost their true identity because of the service they provide for others. For women, their response would be, I am a mother, allowing their role to forsake themselves; a sister, carrying responsibilities for a sibling; a daughter, constantly worrying about the wellbeing of both mom and dad; a woman trying to survive, sometimes working two to three jobs just to make ends meet; I am hard working and dedicated to my family, ensuring that they have everything they need and more.

For men, their response would be, a father, ensuring that my children are well taken care of; a son, being obedient and respectful towards my parents; a provider, certifying that the family maintains a roof over their head, food on the table, clothes on their back; protector, confirming that the family is protected at all times; hard worker, guaranteeing that all the bills are paid and no one has a want or need; head of the house, warranting that he and his house has everything and making tough decisions.

***These are all titles that label a person by what they are. The question is who are you not what are you.***

This is the moment where you begin to describe who God has created you to be. The moment when your inner man needs to speak with pride and say I am a new creation in

Christ, I am the daughter/son of the King of kings. I am royalty, I am who God intended me to be. As you read this, I need you to dig deeper.

You are that important man or woman.

You are that beautiful person with purpose.

God's handiwork, flawless before Him. You are precious and honored in God's eyes. You are valuable to God, created in His image and likeness. Who are you stems deeper than a description given by man. You are the very breath of God. He breathed into you the breath of life.

Before your parents thought of you, God had plans for your life. Jeremiah 1:5 says, "Before I formed thee in the belly I knew thee; and before thou camest forth out of the womb I sanctified thee, I ordained thee a prophet unto the nations."

You are not here by chance.

You are not just an ordinary person. You are who God says you are. Ephesians 1:4 says, "According as he hath chosen us in him before the foundation of the world, that we should be holy and without blame before him in love."

He intentionally molded you and brought you into this world at the exact time you were born. You are not an afterthought. You are not under any circumstances a liability. Genesis 1:27 states, "So God created man in his own image, in the image of God created he him; male and female created he them." God does not make mistakes.

God does not define our identity based upon our status, our race, our titles, or our struggles. Nor does He define our identity based upon our accomplishments, who we know, or do not know. God defines who we are by the relationship we have with Him. We are His chosen people, the ones that He will come back for. The ones that he sacrificed His only Son for. John 3:16-17 says, "For God so loved the world, that He gave His only begotten Son, that whosoever believeth in Him should not perish, but have everlasting life. For God sent not His Son into this world to condemn the world, but that the world through Him might be saved." God proved his loyalty towards us; He has called you His son and daughter.

The reality is the enemy does not want you to know your identity because when you find out who you really are, you defeat the enemy. The power that is inside of you is greater than any attacks the devil will throw against you.

Isaiah 54:17 states, "No weapon that is formed against thee shall prosper; and every tongue that shall rise against thee in judgment thou shalt condemn." The devil will try to get rid of you; he will try to attack you; just know he has already been defeated.

Stand on the promise that God has given to you. If you are not aware of who you are, I encourage you to seek God's face to find out. Spend time praying and fasting before God.

Study God's word. Mark 9:29 says, "And he said unto them, This kind can come forth by nothing, but by prayer and fasting." Matthew 17:21 says, "Howbeit this kind goeth not out but by prayer and fasting." Fasting simply means turning your plate down, sacrificing food to grow closer to God.

You are greater than a title, greater than a label. There was no formula other than God wanting us to be created in His image and likeness. Who are you? You are who God said you are. His beloved child.

# Chapter Nine

# When the spirit Hungers

*There comes a moment when the body grows quiet, and the spirit begins to speak — and that moment is fasting.*

Fasting is more than denying the body; it is feeding the soul. Turning down the volume of the flesh so the voice of God can rise. Throughout Scripture, fasting is a doorway, a bridge between our earthly limitations and divine strength, between human need and heavenly revelation.

Jesus Himself declared the power and purpose of fasting. In Matthew 6:16-18, He taught, *"When ye fast..."* — not **if**, but **when**, revealing that fasting is a normal and expected part of a believer's walk. He instructed us to fast not for attention, recognition, or applause, but in secret, before the Father who sees in secret and rewards openly.

### *Fasting aligns the heart with God's will*

Just to name a few from the Bible:

Ezra fasted for direction.

Esther fasted for deliverance.

Daniel fasted for understanding.

The early church fasted for clarity and commissioning.

And Jesus, before beginning His ministry, fasted for forty days. Proving to us that fasting fortifies, equips, and prepares us for purpose.

There are many ways to fast, each rooted in surrender:

**A food fast** — turning away from meals to feast on prayer.

**A partial fast** — like Daniel, abstaining from certain foods to seek God more intentionally.

**A daily timed fast** — setting aside hours to quiet the flesh and strengthen the spirit.

**A spiritual refocus fast** — laying down distractions, noise, habits, social media, or anything that dulls your sensitivity to God.

The foundation remains the same: Fasting without prayer is only hunger. Fasting without Scripture is only discipline. But fasting with a seeking heart becomes power.

Mark 9:29 reminds us, *"This kind can come forth by nothing, but by prayer and fasting."* Some battles break only when fasting steps in. Some clarity is received only when the body bows low. Some healing comes only when the spirit takes the lead.

**When you fast:**

• Set your intention before God.

• Replace meals or distractions with prayer.

• Meditate on the Word — even if it's just one verse.

• Journal what God reveals.

• End with thanksgiving, not urgency.

Fasting is not a punishment. It's an invitation.

*For when the flesh is silenced, the spirit rises, and in the stillness, you will hear the whisper of the One who satisfies more than bread.*

## Chapter Ten

## When Destiny Calls Your Name

*There comes a moment when the soul rises, shoulders back, chin lifted, and whispers to the world—I am not who I was; I am who God is making me to be.*

Getting to know who you are in Christ is the foundation of true living, but introducing the world to the renewed you becomes the next divine step. People will still look at you through the lens of history, responding to the version of you they first encountered.

Not out of malice, but out of limitation, because they cannot comprehend that the former version of you has died, and the new man has risen. Who you have become is greater than who you were, and for others, familiarity feels safer than your transformation.

This is why you must stand firm. Be confident. Be bold. Be unmoved. It is your time to shine with Heaven's radiance. When you take a stand, you stand against every mindset, influence, memory, and expectation that contradicts who God has called you to be. You are not required to defend your progress. You are not required to shrink to make others comfortable.

**Confidence in Jesus Christ signals clarity, not arrogance.** Philippians 1:6 reminds us that the One who began the work in you will finish it. Next comes holy, supernatural boldness. For God has not given you fear, but power, love, and a sound mind (2 Timothy 1:7). Power equips you to move forward. Love softens your heart toward others. A sound mind guards your thoughts and decisions when pressures arise.

Then comes firmness, an anchored spirit that will not be swayed by opinions, atmospheres, or resistance. I remember the moment God healed me, delivered me, and set me free. When I surrendered, something shifted. The clubs no longer called my name. The desire to drink evaporated. The short skirts and tight dresses were bagged up and passed on.

My speech changed, no longer sharp, impulsive, or reckless. Ephesians 4:29 came alive within me. My appetite changed. My circle changed, and my boundaries strengthened. "No" rolled off my tongue with peace and ease. I laughed more. Smiled more. Lived more. John 8:36 became my reality.

***I was free indeed.***

And this same freedom is available to you. The Holy Spirit works with each person uniquely; comparison has no place in transformation. God meets you where you are. He shapes you gently, grows you intentionally, and reveals Himself consistently. Psalm 73:25 declares that nothing compares to Him. Matthew 6:33 promises that when you seek Him first, everything else aligns.

So, reintroduce yourself. Stand tall, breathe deep, and step forward, because heaven knows your name, purpose crowns your head, and the earth is about to meet the *you* that God Himself awakened.

# Chapter Eleven

## Walking in Your New Identity

*There comes a day when your footsteps must agree with your faith, and your life becomes the evidence of your transformation.*

Up to now, you have rediscovered who you are in Christ. You have confronted insecurity, reclaimed confidence, and learned how God reintroduces you, even to yourself. But identity is not merely something you *realize*. It is something you *walk in*.

### What God awakens must now manifest externally

Walking in your new identity means refusing to return to small thinking, shrinking spaces, and the version of yourself that God has already delivered you from. It means aligning your choices with Truth, not feelings. Scripture calls us to be "doers of the word, and not hearers only" (James 1:22). A renewed identity requires renewed obedience.

This walk is intentional. It shows up in your habits, your thought patterns, the way you speak to yourself, and the way you carry your calling. It means living as someone forgiven, chosen, set apart, strengthened, and loved.

When you stumble, grace lifts you. When doubt whispers, the Spirit reminds you who you are. When fear resurfaces, faith stands taller. To walk in your new identity is to allow the Holy Spirit to shape your behavior, not your past. It is choosing integrity in private and authenticity in public. It is letting transformation be visible, not for applause, but for God's glory. "Since we live by the Spirit, let us keep in step with the Spirit" (Galatians 5:25).

Every step becomes worship when it reflects who God says you are. This identity is not fragile. It does not depend on man's approval, perfection, or performance. It rests on the unchanging character of God. And as you walk in it, your life becomes a testimony—quiet, steady, undeniable.

People begin to see the difference. Peace replaces panic. Purpose replaces drifting. Confidence replaces self-doubt. And the light within you invites others to rise as well.

For the world will always try to call you by who you were, but Heaven will always call you by who you are becoming. Keep walking. Even slowly. Even trembling. Even learning. Trust and believe that your new identity is secure, and every step forward is a declaration that you belong to the One who made you new.

*May your footsteps echo the faith within you, and may your life become the living proof that transformation is real.*

## Chapter Twelve

## The Whisper That Leads the Way

There is a leading that does not shout, a guidance that does not demand, a voice that does not force itself upon the soul, and that is the whisper of God. His whisper is gentle, steady, holy, and unmistakable. It is the voice that awakens you in the stillness of the night, calling you to pray when the world is asleep. It is the nudge that turns your heart, the stirring that interrupts your thoughts. God speaks, not always through thunder or fire, but often through the quiet invitation to come near.

There is something sacred about the hours of **3 and 4 AM**. Those moments when the veil feels thin, when distractions fade, when the noise of the world is silenced. Many believers have experienced it: that sudden waking, that awareness, that pull to get up and pray. It is not anxiety. It is not restlessness.

It is not a coincidence. It is God, gently calling your spirit to His presence.

Isaiah 55:3 declares, *"Incline your ear, and come unto me: hear, and your soul shall live."* God calls your ear first, then your soul awakens. Faith is not born from guessing; it is born from hearing. Romans 10:17 reminds us, *"So then faith cometh by hearing, and hearing by the word of God."* You cannot walk in a path without hearing His direction. You cannot grow in faith without listening to His voice. And you cannot recognize His whisper unless you spend time with Him. The more time you spend in His presence, the more familiar His voice becomes. Just as a child recognizes the voice of a parent, so the believer learns the tone, rhythm, and tenderness of God's leading.

**You Hear God When You Spend Time With Him**

Hearing God is not complicated; it is cultivated. His voice becomes clearer when:

- Your heart is still
- Your mind has surrendered
- Your spirit is open
- Your will is yielded

Time with God trains your spirit to recognize Him: Prayer softens you, worship opens you, The Word aligns you, and silence positions you. You cannot hear God while rushing past Him. You cannot discern Him while living distracted. His whisper is most audible to the heart that lingers. When you spend time with God:

- You stop mistaking fear for warning
- You stop mistaking emotion for direction
- You stop mistaking impulse for urgency
- You stop mistaking opinion for truth

His voice brings **peace**, not confusion. His whisper brings **clarity**, not panic. His leading brings **alignment**, not chaos.

## Why God Speaks in a Whisper

God whispers because:

- He is close
- He desires intimacy
- He draws rather than pushes

- He leads rather than shoves

A whisper requires leaning in. Leaning in requires turning toward Him. Turning toward Him becomes a transformation. Elijah discovered this on the mountain — God was not in the wind, the earthquake, or the fire, but in the still, small voice.

### When God Wakes You to Pray

If God wakes you at night, it may be because:

- Someone needs intercession
- You need strength for what is coming
- He wants to reveal His direction for your life
- Your spirit is being sharpened
- He is aligning you to His will

Some of the greatest spiritual breakthroughs come in the hours no one sees coming.

### Learning to Respond to the Whisper

When God calls you:

- **Pause**
- **Listen**
- **Pray**
- **Write**
- **Obey**

Obedience sharpens discernment. The whisper you honor becomes the voice you trust.

### A Personal Reflection Moment

Have you ever felt that gentle tug? Have you ever been awakened without knowing why? Have you ever felt God drawing you closer? Pause, and think on it. Sometimes His whisper is something you only recognize in hindsight.

### A Poetic Intermission

When God whispers, He does not whisper to your ears but to your spirit. He speaks to the place where fear cannot interfere, where doubt cannot argue, where wounds cannot distort. His whisper is not fragile; it is powerful, steady, life-giving. It is the whisper that parts seas, moves mountains, and heals the broken from the inside out.

### How to Grow in Hearing God's Voice

Here are practices that open the heart:

- Set aside quiet time

- Read Scripture slowly
- Pray without rushing
- Journal impressions
- Sit in silence
- Expect God to respond

God does not hide from those who seek Him. He reveals Himself to the attentive. Let me pause and ask two questions: When have you sensed God speaking the most clearly? How can you create more stillness in your life lately to hear from God?

### Speak This Over Yourself

- My ears are open to God
- I recognize the whisper of the Holy Spirit
- My spirit responds when God calls
- I am led, guided, and directed by the Lord

May your nights become holy ground. May your mornings carry revelation. May your spirit become tuned to heaven. May the whisper of God lead your steps, steady your heart, grow your faith, and draw you deeper into the One who calls you by name even in the stillness of the night.

# Chapter Thirteen

## Becoming Who God Saw All Along

*There comes a moment in every believer's journey when the past can no longer define us, because God whispers a truer identity than we ever dared to believe.*

We spend so many years attracting labels, failure, too much, not enough, broken, inconsistent, and unqualified. The world hands out identities like garments we never asked to wear. But God has always seen beyond what life tried to attach to us. Long before our first breath, before mistakes were made, before insecurity had a voice, **God spoke purpose over us.** He saw who we would become, not in our strength, but in His.

### Defined by God's Love and Purpose

There is a freedom that comes when we realize we were never meant to define ourselves. We were meant to receive an identity shaped by the One who formed us. Scripture reminds us: *"I have been crucified with Christ. It is no longer I who live, but Christ who lives in me…"* — Galatians 2:20.

This means trying to earn others' love ends right here, right now. When Christ lives in us, identity becomes rooted in love, not performance, grace, not perfection. God does not see us through the lens of what we have been, but through the lens of what He placed within us.

Purpose is not something we chase; purpose is something we awaken to. It unfolds as we draw near, as we surrender, as we trust that His design for us is not unstable, temporary, or uncertain.

There are days when transformation feels obvious, and there are days when it feels like nothing has changed at all. But Scripture declares: *"Therefore, if anyone is in Christ, he is a new creation. The old has passed away; behold, the new has come"* — 2 Corinthians 5:17.

**Being Worthy Even When You Don't Feel Worthy**

Many believers secretly wrestle with the same quiet ache:

*"Why would God use someone like me?"*

But worthiness was never earned; it was given. Jesus did not wait for us to be polished, healed, and confident. He chose us knowing every flaw, every hesitation, every moment of doubt. Heaven's calling on your life is not cancelled by insecurity. God is not surprised by the places where you feel small. He meets you there, and He transforms you there.

Becoming who God saw all along means learning to speak to yourself the way God speaks about you:

- Loved
- Redeemed
- Called
- Purposed
- Becoming

Identity in Christ is not a destination reached in a day. Each step of obedience, each moment of surrender, each whisper of faith shapes us more into the person God intended us to be. As we walk with Him, believe Him, and allow His voice to be louder than the world, we rise into the person Heaven has always recognized.

*For you are becoming—not someone different, but someone finally true.*

## Chapter Fourteen

## When Faith Stands in the Fire

Faith is often invisible to the eye, yet it is the strongest force we have in times of trial. It is not built in moments of ease or comfort; it is forged in the heat of life's storms. When the winds rage, the waves rise, and the night feels endless, faith stands in the fire, unshaken, unyielding, and steadfast.

Ephesians 6:12 reminds us, *"For we wrestle not against flesh and blood, but against principalities, against powers, against the rulers of the darkness of this world, against spiritual wickedness in high places."* Our battles are rarely just physical; they are spiritual. The storms we face are often designed to reveal what is truly in our hearts, testing our trust in God, our endurance, and our obedience.

Trials are not punishments; they are refining tools. They mold, shape, and draw us closer to God. Noemí is a profound example of unwavering faith. She lost her husband and her sons, yet she did not abandon God. Through her grief, she held fast, showing us that even in our deepest sorrow, faith can anchor us.

Job's story reminds us of steadfastness under testing. Job lost his wealth, his health, and his children. His friends accused him, suggesting he had sinned to deserve such suffering. Even his wife questioned him, saying, *"Why don't you curse God and die?"*

Yet Job remained steadfast. He did not allow anger, despair, or doubt to control his heart. Instead, he declared, *"Though He slay me, yet will I trust Him"* (Job 13:15). His faith was unseen yet powerful, serving as a beacon to all who read his story.

Even Jesus modeled faith in the midst of storms. While his disciples panicked during a storm at sea, he slept peacefully in the boat. When awakened, He simply said, *"Peace, be still"* (Mark 4:39). His calm authority reminds us that peace is always available when faith rests in God.

Faith requires focus. Peter walked on water as long as his eyes were on Jesus. The moment he looked at the waves and the wind, fear crept in, and he began to sink (Matthew 14:29-30). Faith is not passive; it demands that we fix our eyes on God, even when everything around us seems uncertain.

Jonah's story illustrates that sometimes storms are a divine intervention to capture our attention. Jonah ran from God, attempting to avoid His calling, only to be swallowed by a great fish. The storm was not punishment alone; it was God redirecting him. The lesson is clear: the storms in our lives often come to awaken us, redirect us, or prepare us for the purpose God has for us.

Faith is not about enduring but acting in obedience and trust. The Hebrew boys, Shadrach, Meshach, and Abednego, stood on God's Word in the fiery furnace, refusing to bow to man or compromise their faith. Their courage protected them in the fire because their faith was anchored in the One who saves (Daniel 3:17-18).

David faced relentless trials from Saul, who sought to kill him. For years, David ran for his life. Yet he did not give up. Eventually, he had the opportunity to harm Saul but chose to honor God's timing. David's faith through the storm shaped him into the king God had called him to be. Sometimes, our storms prepare us for the destiny God has already planned.

Faith is unseen, yet it is a form of worship. How we respond to storms reflects the depth of our faith and determines whether we will sink in despair or rise in triumph. God never leaves us nor forsakes us, and He will not place more on us than we can handle.

It is okay to ask God for confirmation, to seek His guidance in prayer, and to ask for a sign. Gideon, doubting his strength and calling, asked God for a sign to confirm His promise

(Judges 6:36-40). Faith, coupled with prayer, is powerful. When we pray with expectation, we align ourselves with God's power, trusting that He is at work behind the scenes. Standing in the fire is not always easy. It requires patience, endurance, and a steadfast commitment to God.

But the reward is growth, wisdom, and spiritual maturity. Remember: your storm is not the end of your story. It is a chapter, not the book. Faith during the fire strengthens the soul, refines character, and draws us closer to God.

It transforms trials into testimonies and strengthens the unseen muscles of trust. The fire may roar, the wind may howl, but your faith anchored in God's promises will stand.

***Faith is not merely believing in God's power; faith is standing firm while the fire surrounds you, confident that the God who began the good work in you will carry it to completion (Philippians 1:6).***

## **Chapter Fifteen**

## **A Life that Shines**

A life that shines is a life that reflects God's presence. It is not measured by wealth, recognition, or popularity, but by the light of God within you. Jesus said in Matthew 5:14, *"Ye are the light of the world. A city that is set on a hill cannot be hid."* You were not created to blend in; you were designed to stand out, to shine bright, to illuminate the path for others. Your life, your conduct, and your faith are visible to the world, and how you walk matters.

One of the clearest indicators of faith is how a person carries themselves. Faith is not merely a belief; it is an action. It is how we respond to challenges, how we treat others, and how we live daily. The fruits of the Spirit, as listed in Galatians 5:22-23—love, joy, peace, patience, kindness, goodness, faithfulness, gentleness, and self-control, are markers of a shining life. When your life reflects these qualities, your faith becomes tangible and observable.

Being a light does not mean dimming your shine to fit in. Too often, we hide our faith, downplay our victories, or shrink ourselves to blend in with the world around us. But God did not call us to conformity. He called us to distinction. Let's look at David. God chose David—a shepherd who was overlooked, underestimated, and disqualified by others—but God saw his potential. He became a king, a man after God's own heart, because he allowed God to work in him, shape him, and shine through him. Like David, your uniqueness is part of God's design.

So how do we become the light? How do we allow our lives to radiate God's presence? The path is simple, though not always easy: **put God first**. Start your day with His Word and end your day with prayer. Meditate on His promises. Memorize scripture, hiding it in your heart so that it guides your actions: *"Thy word have I hid in my heart, that I might not sin against thee"* (Psalm 119:11). Draw near to God, and He will draw near to you (James 4:8).

A shining life also reflects love. Jeremiah 31:3 reminds us, *"Yea, I have loved thee with an everlasting love: therefore with lovingkindness have I drawn thee."* When you allow God's love to flow through you, it becomes visible to those around you. Pray for people, serve them, show kindness, and extend grace. Let the world see God's heart through your words and actions.

Peace is another hallmark of a life that shines. In a world full of chaos, a person guided by God's peace stands out. Their calm demeanor, gentle words, and steady faith reflect the One who sustains them. Living a life that shines is not about perfection—it is about positioning yourself to reflect God's glory. It is about being intentional with your heart, your words, and your actions. It is about walking in the freedom, purpose, and identity that God has given you throughout this journey. Your light is a reflection of God's love, power, and presence. It cannot be ignored, because it is not your light—it is His.

When you let God lead, when you live by His Word, when you reflect His love, your life becomes a beacon of hope and encouragement for others. So live boldly. Love generously. Pray continually. Shine unapologetically. Be the light that the world needs. Out of all your circumstances, trials, and challenges, let your life demonstrate what it means to follow God wholeheartedly.

***Let your life shine not for recognition, but as a testimony of His faithfulness. Be a light that cannot be hidden, a reflection of His glory, a life that points all hearts toward the One who made you to shine.***

## Chapter Sixteen

## The Power of Persistent Prayer

*Prayer is the whisper of the heart that refuses to be silenced, the voice that rises when all else fails, the steady hand that reaches toward heaven without hesitation.*

Persistent prayer is more than a routine; it is a lifestyle. It is the intentional act of drawing near to God, not only when life is easy. When we pray consistently, we are demonstrating faith, dependence, and trust in the One who holds all things in His hands. Prayer is not a suggestion; it is a lifeline.

In Luke 18:1-8, Jesus recounts the parable of the persistent widow. She was a woman who remained steadfast despite facing repeated setbacks. Her persistence was not about forcing God to act; rather, it revealed the posture of her heart. She persisted in knocking, not because God was unaware of her predicament, but because her faith compelled her to continue. In the same way, our faith grows stronger when we refuse to give up, even when the answer seems delayed.

The Bible is filled with examples of persistent prayer that brought God's power into action. Daniel is a prime example. Even under the threat of the lion's den, Daniel did not stop praying three times a day.

His prayers were consistent, disciplined, and full of trust in God. His persistence did not go unnoticed; God's presence was with him during danger, proving that faith paired with persistent prayer is unstoppable.

Another example is Hannah. She fervently prayed for a child. She poured out her heart to God, seemingly unnoticed by others, but God heard her silent cries and answered her faithfulness with Samuel, a prophet who would change the course of Israel's history. Hannah's story reminds us that persistent prayer is about aligning our hearts with God's will, trusting Him to act, and refusing to lose hope.

Faith grows when prayer becomes our first response rather than our last resort. Prayer is a declaration of dependence; it says, "God, I need You, and I trust You. I believe that I am not walking this journey alone." Persistent prayer draws God's presence near, giving you peace in the storm, clarity in confusion, and strength when you feel weak.

### Practical Ways to Cultivate Persistent Prayer

**Set aside specific times each day:** Begin with small blocks of time, five or ten minutes in the morning, or before bed, and gradually build a consistent habit.

**Create a prayer list:** Write down people, circumstances, and personal struggles to pray for. Seeing them on paper helps maintain focus and accountability.

**Use Scripture in prayer:** Praying God's Word over your life strengthens your faith. Verses like Romans 10:17 remind us, "So then faith comes by hearing, and hearing by the word of God." Incorporate God's promises into your prayers.

**Journal your prayers:** Track what you pray for and the ways God answers. Looking back at answered prayers builds confidence and perseverance.

**Pray with others:** Prayer partners or small groups can help maintain persistence and provide encouragement.

Consider modern examples of persistent prayer:

- A single mother praying for a breakthrough in her job search
- A student praying for wisdom and guidance before an exam
- Someone praying for a sick loved one

In every case, persistence demonstrates faith that God is both listening and acting, even if His timing differs from ours. Persistent prayer becomes more vital when facing storms in life. Job lost everything, but he did not curse God. Even when his friends suggested he had sinned, Job stood firm in faith. Noemí, from the book of Ruth, lost her husband and sons, yet she remained faithful to God. These examples teach that trials are not punishments; they are refining processes.

The storm can sometimes be God's way of redirecting our paths, calling us to deeper intimacy with Him. When we approach trials with persistent prayer, we do not allow the storm to define us. Faith and persistent prayer allow us to respond with peace instead of panic, with trust instead of fear. Persistent prayer keeps our eyes fixed on the Lord, strengthening our focus and sustaining our faith.

Jonah ran from God and was swallowed by a great fish, but it caught his attention. Persistent prayer is about remaining connected to God even when we feel lost or overwhelmed. Persistent prayer is also a form of worship. It is not merely asking; it is trusting. Faith is believing when you cannot see, knowing God is working even when circumstances suggest otherwise.

You honor God's power and demonstrate reliance on His timing and wisdom when you pray with persistence. God will never leave you nor forsake you. He will not place more on you than you can bear (1 Corinthians 10:13). It is okay to ask Him for clarity, guidance, and even signs, but do so with a heart of trust, not doubt.

When Gideon asked God for confirmation with the fleece, God met him in faithfulness. Persistent prayer transforms ordinary moments into divine encounters. When you rise early, or linger late into the night, speaking to God, you build a faith that cannot be shaken. When answers seem delayed, your spirit is strengthened, your perspective is shifted, and your heart aligns more closely with His will.

***As you cultivate the power of persistent prayer, you cultivate a faith that sustains, a hope that endures, and a life that experiences God's presence.***

# Chapter Seventeen

# When God Turns Waiting into Becoming

*Some seasons don't demand movement—they demand surrender, for in stillness God shapes what rushing could never build.*

There are moments in the walk of faith when God doesn't say go, run, or speak. He simply says, *WAIT*. And waiting can feel like silence. Delay. Distance. But in the Kingdom of God, waiting is never wasted.

Waiting is where roots grow. Waiting is where trust deepens. Waiting is where faith moves from fragile to unshakable. Isaiah 40:31 declares: *"But they that wait upon the Lord shall renew their strength; they shall mount up with wings as eagles…"*

**Waiting is not God withholding. It is God preparing.**

Think of David. Anointed as king—yet sent back to the field with sheep. Years passed. Battles came. Rejection followed him. But God was teaching him courage, worship, humility, and dependence. Before David carried a crown, he carried a harp. Before he led a nation, he learned to lead himself.

Waiting is where God makes us into what He already sees.

## Faith That Matures in the Quiet

Habakkuk cried out, asking God *when* and *how*. God didn't answer with a date. He answered with a promise: *"Though it tarry, wait for it; it will surely come"* —Habakkuk 2:3.

God is not slow. Delay is often divine training. When the answer doesn't come quickly, faith learns to stand firmly. Sometimes God may not be changing the circumstance, He's changing *you*.

## When Silence Isn't Absence

Heaven may seem still, prayers may feel unanswered, and time may stretch longer than your strength. But silence is not

God leaving you. Silence is God working beyond what your eyes can see. Joseph waited in prison. Elizabeth waited for a child. The disciples waited for the Holy Spirit. Every waiting season birthed a move of God. God's silence is often the doorway to God's glory.

### The Turning Point of Trust

Waiting becomes worship when trust replaces panic. And trust sounds like this: *God, I may not see it, but You are moving. I may not feel it, but You are faithful. I may not know when, but I know Who.* Psalm 27:14 whispers: *"Wait on the Lord: be of good courage, and He shall strengthen thine heart…"* Waiting is not passive. Waiting is warfare. Waiting is choosing faith over fear, peace over panic, purpose over pressure. And then—it happens.

The prayer that felt forgotten becomes fulfilled. The door that never opened swings wide open. The breakthrough that seemed impossible suddenly stands before you. Not because you forced it. Not because you rushed it. But because God did it—at the perfect time. Galatians 6:9 reminds us:

*"In due season we shall reap, if we faint not."* Your due season exists. And God alone holds the calendar. When the promise comes, you will discover something beautiful: You become wiser. Stronger. Calmer. Rooted and built for what God is giving you. The waiting shaped your character to carry the blessing. The blessing didn't make you—it simply revealed what waiting created.

***In the quiet spaces where time stretches, and answers linger, faith learns to breathe—and waiting becomes the place where God turns who you were… into who you were always destined to be.***

## Chapter Eighteen

## Walking in God's Peace

There comes a moment in every believer's life when the battle is loud, but the whisper within becomes louder. A moment when chaos may surround you, but calm begins to rise in you. A moment when you finally realize, peace is not the absence of storms... peace is the presence of God in the middle of them.

Peace is not a feeling you chase. It is a promise you inherit. Jesus did not say, *"I will give you a peaceful life,"* but He did say, *"My peace I give unto you."* (John 14:27). His peace is not fragile. It does not crack under pressure. It does not evaporate when life becomes heavy. His peace stands strong, steady, and unshakable, because it is rooted in Him, not in circumstances.

***When God gives peace, He isn't calming life around you.***
***He's calming life within you.***

Some people assume peace belongs to the quiet, the gentle, the naturally calm. But Scripture tells a different story. Peace is not a personality trait. It is the birthright of every believer. Philippians 4:6-7 declares: "Be anxious for nothing… and the peace of God, which surpasses all understanding, will guard your hearts and minds in Christ Jesus."

Peace doesn't just soothe you—it guards you. It stands like a shield over your heart. It protects your mind from fear. It reminds your spirit that God is still in control. You don't earn peace. You receive it.

The world teaches us to worry first and pray later. God teaches us to pray first and worry never. Peace begins where surrender begins. You don't need to understand everything to have peace. You just need to trust the One who does.

Allow peace to lead you. Peace is more than comfort. It's a direction. Colossians 3:15 says: *"Let the peace of Christ rule in your hearts."* Peace is not passive. Peace speaks.

It says:

- Don't rush
- Wait on God
- This isn't your battle
- Move forward
- He's with you

Peace becomes a compass. It becomes clarity. It becomes confirmation. When you don't know what to do next, follow the peace. If something steals your peace, it is not from God. If something strengthens your peace, God is in it. The safest decisions are the ones led by His peace.

**Peace in the Mind, Peace in the Spirit**

Battlefields are not always physical. Some are quiet. Some are invisible and internal. The enemy fights hardest in the mind because the mind directs the heart, and the heart directs the life:

- Anxious thoughts
- Restless nights
- Racing fears
- Silent battles no one sees

And yet—God's peace reaches even there. Perfect peace is not accidental. It is intentional. You fix your mind on God—and God fixes your peace.

### When Peace Becomes Strength

The world thinks peace is weakness—soft, quiet, passive. But the Word of God says the opposite. Peace is strength. It takes strength to stay calm. Strength to keep quiet when flesh wants to react. Strength to trust when fear screams louder. Strength to believe in God when results are not visible.

*Peace is not the end of faith—Peace is the fruit of faith.*

And when God's peace rests on you, you walk differently. You speak differently. You respond differently.

You stop living shaken and start living anchored.

One of the greatest witnesses of Christ in you is not how loud you share His truth, but how calmly you stand. The world notices the believer who walks in peace when everything around them is falling apart. Peace becomes a testimony. A light. A signal that God is present.

Matthew 5:14 says: *"Ye are the light of the world."* Light is steady. Light is seen. Light does not apologize for shining. You are not called to panic. You are called to shine. Peace is part of that light. The world may chase comfort, but believers carry peace.

### Peace is Proof

If the enemy cannot steal your peace, he cannot steal your purpose. Because peace proves three things:

**1. God is with you**

**2. God is in control**

**3. God will finish what He started**

And when your heart rests in these truths, fear loses its power. Peace is not a place you find; it is God's Presence you walk with. When the storm rises, may your spirit rise higher. When chaos speaks, may faith speak louder. And when life shakes, may you remember—***You are held by the God who never moves.***

Walk in His peace.

Live in His peace.

Breathe in His peace.

*For the One who calmed the seas is the One who calms you.*

## **Closing**

## **The AMEN to Your Becoming**

There comes a moment when the pages stop—but the story does not. This book may close here, but your journey with God is only beginning. You have walked through:

- Healing
- Identity
- Faith
- Fire
- Surrender
- Prayer
- Peace—and every chapter was preparing you for the life God always knew you would live.

You are not who you were. You are who God has called forth. He has been shaping you in silence, strengthening you in storms, whispering to you in the night, and awakening destiny inside of you—chapter by chapter, breath by breath, prayer by prayer.

He saw you before anyone believed in you. He called you before you ever answered. He loved you before you ever understood love.

And now, you stand at the doorway of becoming.

### The God Who Began… Will Finish

What God starts, He sustains.

What God authors, He completes.

What God promises, He performs.

Philippians 1:6 echoes through eternity: *"He who hath begun a good work in you will perform it."* Not might. Not maybe. **Will.**

Your life is not an accident. Your calling is not fragile. Your future is not uncertain. The Author of your story is still writing. Every tear has watered purpose. Every trial has forged strength. Every storm has prepared glory. You have not been breaking—you have been becoming.

### You Are the Light

The world does not need a quieter you. A smaller you. A dimmer you. The world needs *the you,* God designed—**bold**, **steady**, **faithful**, **glowing** with His presence.

*"Ye are the light of the world."* (Matthew 5:14)

Not someday.

Not when you feel ready.

Not when life is perfect.

# Now!

Your light is evidence that Jesus lives in you. Your peace is proof that God walks with you. Your faith is a signal that Heaven is near. Shine anyway. Shine boldly. Shine without apology. For darkness cannot argue with light, it can only flee from it.

### Walk Forward

You don't need to have every answer. You don't need to see the whole road. You don't need to feel strong enough.

All God asks is this—**Take the next step.**

Trust Him. Follow His whisper. Pray without ceasing. Stand in faith. Walk in peace. Live in love.

And when fear tries to pull you backward, remember: You have survived what was meant to break you. You have risen from what was meant to bury you. You have overcome what once overwhelmed you. You are evidence that God is still working miracles.

**This Is Not the End**

This is your release. Your call to rise. Go forward knowing:

- You are chosen
- You are redeemed
- You are equipped
- You are seen
- You are loved
- You are called

Heaven has spoken over you. Purpose is alive in you. The Holy Spirit walks with you. And the God who carried you here will carry you the rest of the way. When the world sees you, may they see the God who ***transformed*** you.

And when your life speaks—may it say what this book has whispered all along:

*Grace found me. Faith changed me. Jesus lives in me. And my story has only just begun.*

*AMEN.*

www.ingramcontent.com/pod-product-compliance
Lightning Source LLC
Chambersburg PA
CBHW071351300426
44114CB00030B/2010